W9-AUZ-212

"Finally, a book about credit scoring that's easy to read and contains accurate information. Three people have already tried stealing my copy."

> ~ *Erica Bracey*
> *Assistant Vice President, Citizens Trust Bank*

"Stephen Snyder has written the clearest and most concise guide I've ever seen on how to take actions today that protect and build your credit scores. He's taken what is usually a very confusing and contrived process and made it easy to understand—in fact this book is actually fun to read. If I were to recommend only one book on how to increase your credit scores—this is the book. No question about it."

> ~ *Scott Mitic*
> *Co-Founder, True Identity, Inc.*

"I loved the book. It is what every consumer needs to know. It takes the myth and mystery out of the process in a concise, enjoyable and easy to understand style. Well done!"

> ~ *Adam Levin*
> *President, Credit.com*

DO YOU MAKE THESE

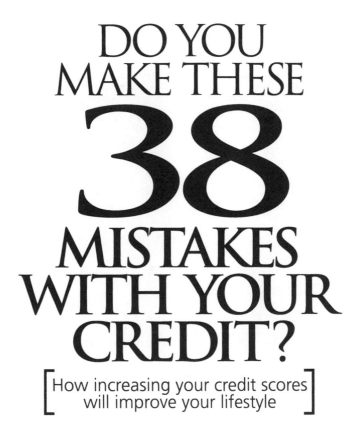

38

MISTAKES WITH YOUR CREDIT?

[How increasing your credit scores will improve your lifestyle]

STEPHEN SNYDER

FICO is a registered trademark of Fair Isaac Corporation.

Published by Bellwether, Inc.
9102 Fallview Drive
Fishers, Indiana 46038-3822

Publisher's Cataloguing-in-Publication Data
Snyder, Stephen.

    Do you make these 38 mistakes with your credit? / by Stephen
    Snyder.—Indianapolis, IN : Bellwether, Inc., 2004, 2005.

    112 p.   1.1 cm.
    ISBN: 1-891945-03-3

    1. Consumer credit—United States. 2. Credit scoring systems—United
    States. 3. Finance, Personal—United States. 4. Credit cards—United
    States. 5. Debtor and creditor—United States. I. Title.

HG3756.U6 S69 2004   2004106527
332.7/43—dc22   0404

Printed in the United States of America
RR Donnelley • Crawfordsville, Indiana
Second edition first printing April 2005
5/10-15

Contents

I would like to thank all my instructors at Fair Isaac Corporation who have helped me understand the subtleties of credit scoring over the years.

∽

Preface

Fifteen years ago it didn't matter. You applied for as much credit as you wanted. And as long as you paid your bills on time, your credit rating was considered good.

That's changed. You are now scored. Lenders now use credit risk scoring to determine whether they will offer you credit and, if you qualify, what interest rate they will extend to you. This score is calculated from information appearing on your credit reports.

The most popular credit score is called the FICO® credit score. A FICO credit score is simply a three-digit number ranging from 300 to 850 that summarizes the information on your credit report.

This score is used by lenders to measure your credit risk. The higher your scores the better.

Lenders have used FICO credit scores to evaluate you for years. Created by Fair Isaac Corporation, FICO credit scores have long been a closely guarded secret kept from consumers.

Until now.

Since June 11, 2003 you can for the first time in history purchase all three of your FICO® credit scores, which enables you to quickly see how lenders see you.

So you purchase your scores…now what?

The next step is understanding how to maintain or increase your FICO credit scores so you can qualify for credit and insurance at the lowest rates with the best terms.

That's what this book is about.

By increasing your FICO credit scores you can:

- Lower your interest rates on your credit cards

- Increase your credit limits

- Save tens of thousands of dollars in interest on a mortgage

- Refinance at a lower interest rate

- Get approved when you would otherwise be denied

- Qualify for a lower car payment

- Get approved for no-money-down financing

- Lower your insurance premiums

- Get utilities without a deposit

- Know whether you will get approved and at what interest rate before you even fill out a credit application

- And more…

This book will touch on the most common mistakes you make with your credit. It is designed to help you create new habits that will quickly increase your credit scores and improve your lifestyle.

Enjoy,

Stephen ☺

Stephen Snyder

Foreword

I've been a part of the consumer credit industry for over 14 years. In that time, I've had the opportunity to read and review no less than 50 books and courses on how to manage and improve credit. Each was billed as the "key to the secret vault" promising to unlock and demystify the secrets behind credit reporting and credit scoring.

Most failed miserably and often contained only marginally accurate information. Worse yet, some of the advice they gave was exactly the opposite of what you should do to maximize your credit standing. If you followed their advice, your credit scores would actually go down instead of up!

The problem is, most of these so-called experts never really had to improve their own personal credit scores. So all they have to offer are untested theories. As such, their books provide little or no information that you could use to increase your credit scores and better manage your credit.

When I finished reading Stephen Snyder's book I let out a deep sigh as I had finally found a book that contained not only accurate information, but also actionable advice. Anyone can tell you to pay your bills on time, but nobody else has captured the little known but valuable facts about credit management contained in this book.

It's obvious that he did his homework and uncovered many techniques and strategies for increasing credit scores that are seldom discussed anywhere else. It's also apparent that he actually used these strategies to increase his personal credit scores.

To top it all off, Mr. Snyder has also done a remarkable job of taking what is often highly technical information and making it easy to understand and implement. He's eliminated all the technical jargon and fancy words and instead writes in a very simple manner anyone can follow.

In an ideal world this book would be required reading before anyone applies for a credit card. I strongly suggest reading this not once, but on a regular basis as you journey through the subtleties of improving your credit.

In today's credit-driven world, whether we like it or not, credit scoring impacts almost every single citizen in the United States. It's critically important for you to maintain high credit scores if you expect to prosper.

And I can't think of a better book to help you than this one.

~John R. Ulzheimer

John Ulzheimer was with Equifax for seven years and the Fair Isaac Corporation for seven years. He has appeared on CNN and Bankrate.com, and also appeared before members of Congress, the Fannie Mae Foundation, the Mortgage Bankers Association, and the National Foundation For Credit Counseling.

Mistake

1

Not Knowing Your Three Credit Scores

Knowing your credit scores is like determining whether you are sick. How do you know if you are sick? Put a thermometer in your mouth and take your temperature. Credit scores are your creditworthiness thermometers.

The first thing you must do is purchase your FICO® credit scores to determine if your credit rating is sick, healthy, or in need of a little attention.

There are a few ways to purchase your FICO credit scores. Refer to the chart on page 83.

Whatever method you use, it all begins by first knowing your scores. Do you know your three FICO credit scores? If not, you really don't know how good or bad your credit is.

Mistake

2

Purchasing the Wrong Scores

Not all credit scores are created equal. Fair Isaac designed and developed credit scoring models that create FICO® scores when credit data is run through them. These models are converted to software and then used at each of the three national credit reporting agencies. This gives each credit reporting agency the ability to provide a FICO score to any lender or consumer who purchases a credit report.

Equifax calls their FICO score a BEACON® score, Experian's is the Experian/Fair Isaac Risk Model®, and TransUnion's is the EMPIRICA® score or FICO Risk Score Classic®. However, don't be fooled. TransUnion and Experian aggressively market their own proprietary consumer credit scores. These scores are meaningless because lenders don't use them.

Make sure you purchase your FICO credit scores. These are the scores lenders use when deciding whether or not to extend you credit.

Mistake

3

Having Unnecessary Credit Inquiries

When you sign a credit application or give a lender your social security number, you give that lender permission to look at your credit report(s).

This appears as a line item on the bottom of your credit report(s) and is commonly referred to as a credit inquiry.

Don't give a lender your social security number or sign a credit application until you know the lender's credit guidelines (refer to Mistake 38). Credit inquiries that you initiate lower your credit scores. If the lender won't tell you their credit guidelines, walk away. It's not worth the risk of a credit inquiry.

Credit inquiries remain on your credit reports for two years. However, they count against your scores for only the first 12 months they appear.

Mistake

Using Lenders That Won't Report Your Credit Limit Accurately

Some credit card companies have made policies not to share your credit limit with the credit reporting agencies. This is a strategic marketing move intended to thwart their competition. Because they don't report your credit limit, competing lenders have no idea just how good a customer you really are and therefore cannot make you a better offer.

Your lenders should report your credit limits to each of the three credit reporting agencies so that your use of each account can be accurately calculated into your FICO® credit scores. If the credit limit for an account you've had in good standing for years is not being reported, your score will not be as high as it could be.

Even worse, some lenders report your current balance as your credit limit. This makes it appear as if you've maxed out your credit limit for a particular account, thus lowering your credit scores.

Mistake

5

Leaving a Balance on Your Credit Cards Each Month

There are many myths circulating about whether or not leaving a balance on your credit card accounts each month improves your credit rating.

The truth is you will receive higher FICO® credit scores if you pay off your credit card balances each month. The closer you get them to a zero balance, the better.

The thing to remember is the lag time it takes each lender to report your balances to the credit reporting agencies. In the worst case, it may take up to 60 days. Unless you stop using the account for two months after you pay it off, you may never see a zero balance on your credit reports.

Mistake

6

Maxing Out Your Credit Cards Each Month

When you max out your credit card limit or even come close to doing so, you appear more risky to a lender and your credit scores suffer.

If you want to increase your credit scores fast, pay off your credit card balances each month.

Mistake

7

Assuming Your Lenders Share Your Payment History with the Credit Reporting Agencies

Our credit reporting system in the United States is a voluntary system. This means lenders are not required to report your payment history to the three national credit reporting agencies.

Credit unions are the worst offenders. The majority of credit unions choose not to report your payment history to all three national credit reporting agencies.

If your lenders are not reporting your excellent payment history, your FICO® credit scores will not be as high as they could be.

Mistake

Rate Shopping
the Wrong Way

There is an art to shopping for the best interest rate.

Fair Isaac tries to model your shopping experience. For example, if you have seven car-related credit inquiries in a short period of time, they realize that you are not buying seven cars. They know you're rate shopping.

Because having too many credit inquiries on your credit report will lower your FICO® credit scores, you should do all your shopping for a car loan or a mortgage within a 14-day time period. Here's the loophole: all credit inquiries for car loans or mortgages within this time period will count as only one credit inquiry.

This time period will be extended to 45 days by 2006.

Mistake

9

Acquiring Your Credit Reports from a Third Party

You should only acquire your credit reports directly from the three national credit reporting agencies to avoid unnecessary credit inquiries.

Credit reports acquired directly from Equifax, Experian, and TransUnion will *not* lower your FICO® credit scores. A credit report sent via regular mail from each credit reporting agency is more complete than credit reports available online. And remember, your credit reports will *not* have your FICO credit scores on them.

If you want your FICO credit scores, the best place to purchase them is through www.myfico.com/12. Ordering from this site will *not* lower your FICO credit scores.

Mistake

10

Using Finance Companies

There is a difference in the type of lenders you use.

Banks and credit unions are looked at more favorably from a FICO® credit scoring standpoint than general finance companies. A few examples of general finance companies to avoid are American General Finance, Beneficial, CitiFinancial, Heights Finance Corporation, Lendmark Financial Services, and World Acceptance Corporation.

Having a general finance company account on your credit report will lower your FICO credit scores.

Choose your lenders wisely.

Mistake

11

Closing Accounts

Closing accounts can have a negative impact on your credit scores in two ways.

The immediate effect: Let's say you have 10 credit cards, each with a $1,000 limit. You've maxed out five of the cards and you haven't used the other five for years. If you close the five unused accounts, your total credit card limit will immediately be maxed out and your scores will suffer dramatically. However, by not closing those five unused accounts you are using only 50% of your available credit.

The long-term effect: Closing accounts that have been open for years, unused or not, shortens your credit history and lowers your credit scores. When you close a credit account, the clock begins ticking to determine how much longer that account's history will remain on your credit reports.

The key to obtaining high credit scores is to manage your credit accounts well over an extended period of time.

Mistake

12

Believing That "Ka-Ching" Can Overcome Everything

Your income has nothing to do with your credit scores.

The exception to this rule is if the lender is still using an "application score" based on information provided on your credit application. This is how lenders decided to extend credit years ago before FICO® credit scoring became popular.

But for the most part, the fact that you have a high income, were promoted, received a raise, or earned a hefty bonus at the end of the year doesn't mean lenders will overlook low or bad credit scores.

Income is a measurement of capacity (e.g., the ability to make your monthly house payment). Creditworthiness, on the other hand, is based on whether or not you choose to make the payment.

Remember, it's all about your credit scores.™

Mistake

Ignoring the Relationship Between Your Credit Reports and Your Insurance Rates

Your credit reports influence more than just the credit decisions lenders make.

Most insurance companies now use information appearing on your credit reports to determine whether you get insurance. And if you currently have auto or homeowners insurance, low credit scores may increase your insurance premiums.

Most of the insurance industry is regulated at the state level. Each state creates its own laws dictating how insurance companies can use information appearing on your credit reports.

To determine where your state government stands on this issue go to www.namic.org/reports/credithistory/creditlaws.asp

Mistake

14

Thinking a Bank Debit Card Helps Your Credit Rating

Debit cards are convenient, but they will not help you increase your credit scores.

Although debit cards have Visa® or MasterCard® logos, they are not actual credit cards. They are really nothing more than a plastic check.

Since there is no credit extended, the debit card account will not appear on your credit reports. Only information appearing on your credit reports is considered in calculating your FICO® credit scores.

Mistake

15

Co-signing for Another Person

Co-signing for another person is risky any way you look at it.

If the person for whom you co-sign defaults, you are still held responsible for making timely payments. Any late payments will also be recorded on your credit reports and will lower your credit scores.

In addition, if the loan appears on your credit reports it may affect your debt-to-income ratios and limit your ability to qualify for the credit you need.

It's best not to co-sign for anyone. Loan them cash, not your credit.

Mistake

16

Using Cash Only

Paying cash for everything used to make sense, but credit scoring has changed that.

Lenders need to see that you can pay your bills on time. If nothing appears on your credit reports because you have been paying with cash only, you may be denied credit. Even worse, you may not have the minimum credit history to even receive a credit score from each credit reporting agency.

The minimum information you need on each credit report to receive a credit score is one credit account that has been open for six months and one credit account that has been updated by a creditor within the past six months.

Remember, paying cash for things does not increase your credit scores.

Mistake

17

Allowing a Collection Account to Appear on Your Credit Reports

The appearance of a collection account on your credit reports lowers your credit scores. Paying the balance will not increase your credit scores.

> WARNING: Even if you pay the balance of the collection account after it appears on your credit reports, the paid collection account will continue to lower your credit scores for up to seven years.

Before you pay off an inaccurate, outdated, or unverifiable collection account, try negotiating with the lender to remove the account as part of the settlement. If the collection account is removed, your credit scores will increase significantly.

Mistake 18

Applying for a Home Equity Line of Credit (HELOC)

There is a subtle difference between a home equity loan and a home equity line of credit (HELOC). The difference is how they appear on your credit reports and impact your FICO® scores.

A home equity loan is safer because it will report as an installment trade line.

A home equity line of credit may be considered part of your revolving debt, which could wreak havoc on your FICO credit scores if you carry a high balance.

Avoid HELOCs. Use home equity loans instead.

Mistake

19

Transferring Credit Card Balances to Get a Better Interest Rate

On the surface this seems like a smart move. You save money. But transferring credit card balances may in fact lower your credit scores.

Transferring balances just shifts debt. Shifting debt doesn't increase your credit scores. Since your debt is calculated in total, you should instead focus on paying down debt with the goal of paying it off each month.

When you transfer balances to a new credit card, you initiate a new credit inquiry and create a new account, both of which lower your scores. Then, if the new lender requires the previous lender to close the account, your scores will eventually be lowered again (refer to Mistake 11).

Mistake

Having Too Many Credit Inquiries

Every time you apply for credit by filling out a credit application or giving a lender your social security number, a credit inquiry appears on each credit report the lender pulls.

Applying for a lot of new credit accounts in a short period of time is a red flag to lenders. They may perceive you as someone who will become over-extended by acquiring credit beyond your means. The exception is when you apply for mortgage or car loans (refer to Mistake 8).

It is especially important not to make this mistake during the holiday season, when retail stores tempt you with discount offers if you apply for their credit card. Ignore them. Sure, you'll save money on your purchases, but the credit inquiries will lower your credit scores and could make something like refinancing your mortgage more expensive.

Mistake

21

Not Having
Major Credit Cards

People without major credit cards are considered a higher risk than people who have major credit cards.

To increase your credit scores, maintain a few major credit cards over a long period of time.

Ideally, you should use a Visa® or MasterCard® issued by a bank or an American Express® or Discover® Card. A card offered through a credit union is just as good, as long as they report to all three national credit reporting agencies.

Mistake

22

Paying Off Installment Credit Accounts Early

U nlike a revolving account where the monthly payment varies with your balance, installment loans are usually made with a specific number of payments over a specific number of months.

The longer you hold an installment account in good standing, the higher your credit scores.

So keep that installment loan on your car for the full term of the loan. Likewise, keep your mortgage for the full term or as long as it makes sense before you refinance.

Again, you'll earn the highest FICO® credit scores when you manage your accounts well over a long period of time.

Mistake

23

Ignoring Your "Negative Reason Codes"

Each of your FICO® credit scores from the three national credit reporting agencies is accompanied by four two-digit negative reason codes for a total of 12 codes.

In a lot of ways, your 12 negative reason codes are more important than your scores. These reason codes explain why your credit scores are not as high as they could be. They also offer guidance on how to increase your individual credit scores.

How do you get your negative reason codes for all three of your FICO credit scores? Go to www.myfico.com/12 or refer to the chart on page 83.

Mistake

24

Improperly Dividing Debt in a Divorce

A divorce decree does not change the fact that you are a co-borrower on a loan. What typically happens is a couple divides their debt with no regard for who is legally responsible for the debt. Each person is still responsible regardless of what the judge says.

Both co-borrowers will suffer if one borrower defaults. So it's best to assume responsibility for all debt for which you were a co-borrower. This will ensure your credit is not negatively affected.

If you are unable to assume responsibility for all co-borrowed debt, it's best to close the accounts. If you have accounts that you cannot close, refinance them to put them in one person's name. Closing accounts in this situation is the lesser of two evils. It will lower your scores, but it's better than repeatedly making late payments (refer to Mistakes 11 and 36).

You should also contact your lenders to determine what other options you have.

Mistake

25

Not Increasing Your Credit Limits

Increasing your credit limits is one of the fastest and easiest ways to increase your credit scores.

When you increase your credit limits and your spending patterns remain the same you end up using a smaller percentage of your combined credit limits. This increases your scores.

Make it a practice to ask for higher credit limits on a regular basis, usually every six months. When you ask lenders for a credit limit increase, the resulting credit inquiry will lower your scores, but a credit inquiry is usually less damaging than a maxed out credit limit.

Lenders periodically review your account to determine whether or not to increase your credit limit. This type of credit inquiry will not lower your scores.

Mistake

26

Ignoring Mistakes on Your Credit Reports

Having inaccurate, outdated, or unverifiable information on your credit reports can prevent you from getting the credit you need or make the credit you get more expensive.

Since all information appearing on your credit reports affects not only your credit scores, but also your insurance premiums (refer to Mistake 13), it's important to review your credit reports on a regular basis to look for errors.

You can do this yourself or hire an attorney to do it for you.

Mistake

27

Applying for Credit at the Wrong Time

If you plan to buy a home or refinance soon, don't apply for any other credit until *after* you close the mortgage.

Some mortgage lenders will look at your credit scores twice—at the time of application and before the loan closes—to be sure everything has remained the same or improved.

Mistake

Having "Negative Narratives"

Negative narratives are negative comments lenders put on your credit report concerning your account. Most "negative narratives" lower your credit scores.

The most common "negative narratives" are:

- Charge-offs

- Accounts included in wage earner plan

- Accounts included in bankruptcy

- Repossessions (voluntary or involuntary)

- Settlements accepted on an account

Work with the lender to resolve any "negative narratives" or hire an attorney to represent you.

Mistake

29

Using Your Personal Credit for Your Business

If you're an entrepreneur, it's important that you separate your personal credit from your business credit.

Acquire a few business credit cards. Most business credit cards do not report to your personal credit reports. So your use of these cards will not affect your personal credit scores.

Since some credit unions don't report to all three national credit reporting agencies, you may use credit cards from them with the same result.

Mistake

30

Believing You Can Force a Creditor to Report Your Payment History

You have credit, but you discover that your lender does not report your payment history to the three national credit reporting agencies.

Ask them to report. If they ignore your request, find a lender that does report to all three national credit reporting agencies. Remember, lenders are not obligated to report.

Obviously, if your credit with a lender is bad, it's best that they *don't* report to the credit reporting agencies.

Mistake

31

Believing in a Debt Consolidation Loan

The problem with a debt consolidation loan is that it frees you up to spend more.

A debt consolidation loan can pay off all your credit cards, but it also puts you in a position to use them again. And whammo, you're back in the red—twice over.

In general, you should stay away from debt consolidation loans. The only exception is if you consolidate using a home equity loan. Since this may be tax deductible, it could make sense. But you run the risk of losing your home if you default.

The best use of a home equity loan is for real estate investment. For more information go to www.38mistakes.com/resources

Mistake

32

Accepting
Preapproved Offers

Preapproved doesn't mean approved.

Look closely at the credit application. If the lender asks for your social security number, they need to pull your credit report. So you're not actually approved. You're conditionally approved, which essentially means nothing.

The big print giveth and the small print taketh away. Read the fine print. Does it mention that the lender has the right to pull your credit reports? Does it guarantee a certain credit amount? Do the words "up to" appear when referring to the credit line you expect?

Contact each lender and ask for their credit guidelines before you apply (refer to Mistake 38).

Mistake

33

Adding a Consumer Statement to Your Credit Reports

Under the Fair Credit Reporting Act, you have the right to add a 100-word consumer statement to your credit reports to explain any information that appears on them (refer to page 81). Some states allow consumers to add a 200-word statement.

Don't do this. Consumer statements are not taken into account as part of your credit scores.

Few lenders, if any, really care about the statement. Most don't read it. Remember, lenders use credit scores. Either your credit scores qualify you or they don't.

In addition, you may end up verifying negative information about your credit history. Forget the consumer statement and simply communicate with your lender or hire an attorney to represent you.

Mistake

34

Having Credit, But Not Using It

Having credit accounts and not using them can impact your credit scores.

To achieve the highest credit scores you need to use your credit accounts. When your accounts lie dormant they may be closed at the lender's discretion and will eventually disappear from your credit reports (refer to Mistake 11).

The ideal scenario is to use your credit accounts and pay them off each month.

Mistake

35

Not Having
a Mortgage

Renters are perceived as a higher risk than homeowners in the eyes of many lenders.

To achieve the highest credit scores you need a mortgage. It's a sign of stability.

Mistake

36

Having Recent
Late Payments

Late payments have the most significant negative impact on your FICO® credit scores. However, there are different levels of negative. Recent and frequent late payments will hurt you more than an isolated late payment two or more years ago.

What is a late payment? Any bill that reports to the national credit reporting agencies that is late 31 or more days from the due date.

If you are running short any given month, do whatever possible not to be late on any accounts that are reported to the three national credit reporting agencies. How do you know what is reported? Simple—read your credit reports.

Mistake

37

Having Too Much of One Thing

It's best to have a healthy mix of credit.

An ideal scenario would include some installment loans from a bank or credit union that reports to all three credit reporting agencies, a few major credit cards, and one or two retail credit cards.

You will not obtain the highest credit scores by having only one type of credit (e.g., only retail credit cards).

Mistake

38

Not Asking for a Lender's Credit Guidelines Before You Apply for Credit

Most people just apply for credit and hope for the best. As an informed consumer, you should ask specific questions about what the lender needs to get you approved.

You do this to avoid unnecessary credit inquiries, which can lower your credit scores (refer to Mistake 3).

The four most important questions that will help you understand a lender's credit guidelines are:

1. What credit reporting agency do you use when making a credit decision?

2. What is the minimum FICO® credit score you require to get approved?

3. What is the minimum FICO® credit score you require to get approved at your best interest rate?

4. How does a "little bugaboo" affect your lending decision? Since most of us have a "little bugaboo" on our credit reports that we fear the lender will discover, you need to address this up front.

By asking these questions, getting answers to them, and comparing lenders' requirements with your own FICO credit scores, you can know whether you will get approved before you apply. This is especially important with a mortgage, major credit card, or new car loan.

If a lender refuses to answer your questions, move on to the next lender to avoid an unnecessary credit inquiry.

Work with lenders that use the credit reporting agency with your highest FICO credit score to get the best interest rate.

In Closing

You've just read 38 mistakes to avoid that will help you increase your credit scores.

So, what should you do now?

First of all, you need to purchase your FICO® credit scores and reason codes. The best way is through www.myfico.com/12.

As you begin charting your progress toward achieving higher FICO credit scores, it's important to purchase your scores from the same source each time for comparison purposes. Not all sources use the most current version of the software that calculates FICO credit scores.

FICO credit scores are not available free and the only way to obtain them is to purchase them.

When approaching lenders your best plan of attack is to know which credit reporting agency has given you the highest FICO score and look for lenders that exclusively use that score.

However, this doesn't apply when shopping for a mortgage. The majority of mortgage lenders use what is known as your "middle score." They ignore your highest and lowest scores and use the one in the middle.

Your scores will vary between credit reporting agencies for many reasons. The biggest reason is that some lenders do not report to all three national credit reporting agencies. So information will vary, causing different scores.

Also keep in mind that Fair Isaac Corporation (the creators of the FICO® credit score) updates their scoring models about every two years. For example, mortgage and auto credit inquiries made within a 45-day time period will soon only count as one credit inquiry. This is great news for rate shoppers. In addition, the minimum scoring criteria will be expanded to allow more people to be scored.

As I was writing this book, a new statement was added to mortgage lenders' credit reports. If your score was affected by credit inquiries, your mortgage lender is now required to disclose this during the mortgage process.

Another hot issue is how employers look at credit reports when making a hiring decision. Is this legal? Yes.

Employers have guidelines they must follow before they can look at your credit reports. To learn more refer to the link on page 81 where you can read Section 604 of the Fair Credit Reporting Act.

Increasing your credit scores is important. High scores will give you access to the lifestyle you once had or have always dreamed about. I hope this book has given you a jump start on learning how to increase or maintain your scores.

If you would like more in-depth information on how to increase your credit scores, refer to the resources starting on the next page.

May you attain and maintain scores over 750.

Appendix

Resources

How To Purchase Your Credit Scores
See chart on page 83.

How To Purchase Your Credit Reports
See chart on pages 84-85.

How To Get Your Credit Reports Free
A new law called the Fair and Accurate Credit Transactions Act (FACTA) allows you to get one free copy of your credit report from each of the three national credit reporting agencies on an annual basis.

For more information about ordering your reports go to www.annualcreditreport.com or call 1-877-322-8228.

Increase Your Credit Scores
Improve Your Lifestyle™
This step-by-step home study course shows you everything you need to know to improve your credit scores and get approved for the credit and insurance you need. The detailed course manual offers in-depth instructions on how to increase your credit scores to qualify for the lowest possible interest rates and the best terms. In addition, the course includes free access to the Credit Scoring Hotline™, where you can get answers to all your credit scoring questions via telephone or e-mail.

For more information call 1-317-595-3696 or
go to www.increaseyourcreditscores.com

For the most current resources go to
www.38mistakes.com/resources

The Fair Credit Reporting Act (FCRA)

The Fair Credit Reporting Act protects your rights concerning your personal credit reports. It requires credit reporting agencies to report information accurately and to remove or correct information appearing on your credit reports that is inaccurate, outdated, or unverifiable.

To download the FCRA go to www.ftc.gov/os/statutes/fcrajump.htm and follow these steps:

1. Scroll to the bottom of the page.
2. Click on the Fair Credit Reporting Act link in the Major Links box.

The Fair and Accurate Credit Transactions Act (FACTA)

The FACT Act updates the FCRA and allows you to get one free copy of your credit reports annually. To download FACTA go to www.ftc.gov/os/statutes/fcrajump.htm and follow these steps:

1. Scroll to the bottom of the page.
2. Click on the Fair and Accurate Credit Transactions Act of 2003 link in the Major Links box.
3. Go to Latest Major Action: Became Public Law No: 108-159 [GPO: Text, PDF]. Click on Text or PDF.

The Credit Repair Organizations Act (CROA)

The Credit Repair Organizations Act contains the legal guidelines used by reputable firms that dispute inaccurate, outdated, and unverifiable information with the credit reporting agencies on behalf of a consumer.

To download a copy of the CROA go to www.ftc.gov/os/statutes/croa/croa.htm

Higher Credit Scores Save You Money

To compare current rates in your state go to
www.38mistakes.com/savemoney

MORTGAGE LOAN EXAMPLE

The chart below shows how a higher FICO® credit score would save you
money on a 30-year fixed mortgage loan for $150,000.

FICO Score	APR*	Monthly Payments	Total Interest Paid
720-850	5.785%	$879	$166,331
700-719	5.910%	$891	$170,639
675-699	6.447%	$943	$189,437
620-674	7.597%	$1,059	$231,169
560-619	8.531%	$1,157	$266,400

AUTO LOAN EXAMPLE

The chart below shows how a higher FICO® credit score would save you
money on a 60-month auto loan for a new automobile that costs $25,000.

FICO Score	APR*	Monthly Payments	Total Interest Paid
720-850	5.413%	$477	$3,592
690-719	6.213%	$486	$4,148
660-689	8.296%	$510	$5,628
625-659	10.595%	$539	$7,311
590-624	14.287%	$585	$10,126

* Information above calculated as of March 2005.

The rates shown are averages based on thousands of financial lenders, conducted daily by Informa Research
Services, Inc. The 60-month new auto loan APRs are estimated based on the following assumptions: a loan amount
between $10,000 and $20,000, 60 months, and interest rates are fixed for the term of the loan. (Variable rate loans
may be available but are not usually beneficial to a consumer in a low interest rate environment.)

How to Purchase Your FICO® Credit Scores

FICO® Scores Provider (alpha order)	Mortgage Company	www.myfico.com	www.myfico.com/12	www. whataremycreditscores.com 1-800-575-4182 (orders only)
Stephen's Recommendation	★ May be a viable option if you've already applied for a mortgage.	★★ Navigation can be a bit confusing. Only 4 of 12 negative reason codes are provided.†	★★★★★ Site exclusively sells 3 FICO scores. Includes all 12 negative reason codes lenders use.†	★★★★ Convenient ordering methods, payment options, and lower cost.
Cost	$50.00*	$44.85	$44.85	$29.00
Order Method	Direct	Web Only	Web Only	Phone, Fax, Mail or Email
Payment Method	Varies	Credit Card Required	Credit Card Required	Check, Credit Card, or Money Order
Effect of Credit Inquiry	May Lower Scores Short-Term**	Scores Unaffected	Scores Unaffected	May Lower Scores Short-Term**
Purchase Experience	Varies	Security Questions	Security Questions	Just Sign Form
Delivery	Days	Immediate	Immediate	Immediate or Days
All Negative Reason Codes† Provided	Yes	No	Yes	Yes
Report Explaining All Negative Reason Codes	No	No	Yes	Yes Plus More††

* Cost varies. Actual cost may be higher or lower depending on mortgage company.
** Score is unaffected if you apply for mortgage or bank credit within 14 days of purchasing scores.
† Negative Reason Codes are 12 additional codes (4 per FICO credit score) that give you specific information on why your score isn't as high as it could be and what to do about it.
†† Plus More: Additional information on how your current scores compare in different types of lending situations.
FICO is a registered trademark of Fair Isaac Corporation.

How to Purchase Your Credit Reports

The best way to get your credit reports is to purchase them from the three national credit reporting agencies directly and have them mailed to you. The charts to the right show the fees (as of March 2005) to purchase your reports, contact information to order, and materials you will need to send with your order.

The fees fluctuate from time to time. To see the most current information go to www.purchasemyreports.com

Please note: The consumer reports that you receive will not include your FICO®credit scores. You need to purchase your FICO credit scores separately (see the chart on page 83).

EQUIFAX

How to get your Equifax report:
▶ Cost:

State Fees:	
California: $8.00	
Colorado, Massachusetts: One free report per calendar year	
Connecticut: $5.00	
Georgia: Two free reports per calendar year	
Maine, Maryland, New Jersey, Vermont: One free report per 12 month period	
Minnesota: $3.00	
Montana: $8.50	
All other states: $9.50	

▶ Phone Ordering Instructions:
To order over the phone, dial
1-800-685-1111

▶ Mail Ordering Instructions:
    Equifax Information Services LLC
    PO Box 740241
    Atlanta, GA 30374

You must draft a letter with the following info:
• Full name (including Jr., Sr., III)
• Date of birth
• Social security number
• Current street address (apt.#), city, state, zip code
• Previous addresses in past 5 years
• Proof of your current address (e.g., copy of driver's license or utility bill.)
• Phone number
• Signature
• Applicable fee in check or money order payable to Equifax

experian®

How to get your Experian report:
► Cost:

State Fees:
California: $8.00
Colorado, Massachusetts, New Jersey: One free report per calendar year
Connecticut: $5.30 for first report in calendar year
Georgia: Two free reports per calendar year
Hawaii: $9.88
Maine, Maryland, Vermont: One free report per 12 month period
Minnesota: $3.00
Montana: $8.50
New Mexico, South Carolina: $9.98
New York, Texas: $10.28
Pennsylvania: $10.17
South Dakota, West Virginia: $10.07
Washington DC: $10.05
All other states: $9.50

► Phone Ordering Instructions:

For instruction to receive your Experian report via mail, dial 1-888-397-3742

► Mail Ordering Instructions:
Experian
PO Box 2104
Allen, TX 75013

You must draft a letter with the following info:
• Full name (including middle initial, Jr., Sr., III)
• Date of birth
• Social security number
• Spouse's full name and social security number
• Current street address (apt.#), city, state, zip code
• Previous addresses in past 5 years
• Two proofs of your current address (e.g., copies of driver's license, utility bill, bank statement, phone bill, insurance statement, etc.)
• Phone number
• Signature
• Applicable fee in check or money order payable to Experian

Trans**Union**™

How to get your TransUnion report:
► Cost:

State Fees:
California: $8.00
Colorado, Massachusetts: One free report per calendar year
Connecticut: $5.00
Georgia: Two free reports per calendar year
Maine, Maryland, New Jersey, Vermont: One free report per 12 month period
Minnesota: $3.00
Montana: $8.50
Virgin Islands: $1.00
All other states: $9.50

► Phone Ordering Instructions:

For instructions to receive your TransUnion report via mail, dial 1-800-888-4213

► Mail Ordering Instructions:
TransUnion
Consumer Disclosure Center
PO Box 1000
Chester, PA 19022

You must draft a letter with the following info:
• Full name (first, middle, last, including Jr., Sr., III)
• Date of birth
• Social security number
• Current street address (apt.#), city, state, zip code
• Previous addresses in the past 2 years
• Proof of your current address (e.g., copy of driver's license, utility bill, bank statement, lease, W-2, etc.)
• Current employer
• Phone number
• Signature
• Applicable fee in check or money order payable to TransUnion

Get answers to your
credit scoring
questions
FAST

"Welcome to the Credit Scoring Hotline™. What question may I help you with today?"

Sometimes it's easier just to call someone for help. That's what the Credit Scoring Hotline is all about. You call. You get the right answer to your question. It's that simple.

And if for some reason we don't have the answer to your specific question we will research it further with Fair Isaac Corporation and get back in touch with you within 48 hours.

Now answers to your credit questions are finally within reach. Call the Credit Scoring Hotline today.

For more information call us at
1-317-595-3696
Email: pam@creditscoringhotline.com

Increasing Your Credit Scores Saves You Money

With higher credit scores, banks, car dealerships, mortgage companies, and other lenders are more likely to extend you credit at the lowest possible interest rates. By knowing your 12 negative reason codes you will understand why your scores are not as high as they could be and what you can do to increase them.

Myfico.com/12 is the only place where you get all three of your FICO credit scores, a detailed report explaining your scores, and most importantly, your 12 negative reason codes that lenders see.

It's fast and simple to get all three of your FICO credit scores and all 12 negative reason codes. Go online today to www.myfico.com/12.

www.myfico.com/12

This credit inquiry will NOT lower your credit scores

Free
Loan Calculator

www.38mistakes.com/savemoney

Who Uses FICO® Credit Scores?

99 of the 100 largest banks in the United States...

49 of the 50 largest U.S. credit card issuers...

More than 400 insurance companies...

More than 150 retailers...

9 of the top 10 retail card issuers in the United States...

More than 80 government or public agencies...

More than 100 telecommunications carriers...

The top 10 U.S. wireless providers...

Information obtained from www.fairisaac.com/Fairisaac/Company/Clients